The Story of the TITANIC

By Deborah Heiligman
Illustrated by James Watling

A Random House PICTUREBACK® Book

Text copyright © 1998 by Deborah Heiligman. Illustrations copyright © 1998 by James Watling. All rights reserved under International and Pan-American Copyright Conventions. Published in the United States by Random House, Inc., New York, and simultaneously in Canada by Random House of Canada Limited, Toronto.

Library of Congress Cataloging-in-Publication Data
Heiligman, Deborah. The story of the Titanic / by Deborah Heiligman.   p. cm.
SUMMARY: Describes the disastrous maiden voyage of the Titanic, "the safest ship ever built," which sank after colliding with an iceberg in the spring of 1912.   ISBN: 0-679-88808-X (pbk.) — ISBN: 0-679-98808-4 (lib. bdg.)
1. Titanic (Steamship) – Juvenile literature. 2. Shipwrecks – North Atlantic Ocean – Juvenile literature. [1. Titanic (Steamship). 2. Shipwrecks.] I. Title. G530.T6H45 1998 363.12'3'09631 – dc21 97-47275
www.randomhouse.com/kids/
Printed in the United States of America 10 9 8 7 6 5 4 3 2 1
PICTUREBACK is a registered trademark of Random House, Inc.

For my unsinkable sister, Linnie—D. H.

For Liza—J. W.

On April 10, 1912, a large crowd came to watch a new ship, the *Titanic*, set sail from England on her first voyage.

The *Titanic* was the biggest and fanciest ship ever built. It was almost 900 feet long— as long as three football fields. It had a gym, a swimming pool, elegant dining rooms, three libraries, five grand pianos, a squash court, and even a hospital with an operating room.

The *Titanic* also had special watertight compartments below. If the ship hit something that punctured the hull, the captain would just push a button. Doors would then close, sealing off the hole and keeping the water out of the main part of the ship so it wouldn't sink. The *Titanic* was said to be the safest ship ever built. It was said to be *unsinkable*.

At noon, with a loud blast of its horn, the *Titanic* set sail for New York.

For the next few days, Captain E. J. Smith and his crew were busy running the ship. The passengers were busy making friends, playing games, listening to music, and eating lots of good food.

On the evening of April 14, the first-class passengers had a delicious dinner of oysters, roast duckling, and lamb, with chocolate eclairs for dessert. If you were in second class, you might have had plum pudding or ice cream, instead—or both!

The passengers were having so
much fun that they did not worry about
ice or accidents or danger at sea. They
did not know that other ships were
sending the *Titanic* warnings about ice
in the water ahead. They did not know
that the warnings were being ignored
by the *Titanic's* crew.

At 9:20 p.m., Captain Smith went to bed. He gave orders for his crew to wake him if there was any trouble. But he did not give any orders to slow down because of the ice. He was trying to sail across the Atlantic Ocean faster than any ship had before. Indeed, the *Titanic* was moving very quickly.

Up in the crow's nest, the lookouts tried to keep warm and to watch for ice as best they could. They should have had binoculars to help them spot danger far away, but there were not enough on board. The lookouts stared ahead into the darkness.

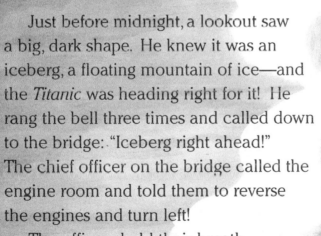

Just before midnight, a lookout saw
a big, dark shape. He knew it was an
iceberg, a floating mountain of ice—and
the *Titanic* was heading right for it! He
rang the bell three times and called down
to the bridge: "Iceberg right ahead!"
The chief officer on the bridge called the
engine room and told them to reverse
the engines and turn left!

The officers held their breath.

But the ship could not turn fast
enough. The *Titanic* hit the iceberg.

Captain Smith and Thomas Andrews, the man who had designed the *Titanic*, went down below to look at the damage. Would the watertight compartments save the ship? No, said Andrews. Six of the sixteen watertight compartments had already started filling up. Water was gushing into the ship. It was going to go down. The *Titanic,* the greatest ship ever built, the safest ship on the seas, was going to sink on its first voyage.

As water poured into the ship, the *Titanic* sent the same message over and over again: *SOS—HELP!* The captain and crew waited for replies from nearby ships. Would anyone be able to help?

The *Carpathia*, an ocean liner traveling from New York to the Mediterranean, radioed back that it could be there in four hours. But Captain Smith knew that would not be soon enough. The *Titanic* was going to sink in about two hours.

The captain and crew saw the lights of a ship close by. It had not answered their SOS calls. So they fired rockets into the air. The rockets were another signal that meant "Help!" But the ship did not answer. The *Titanic* signaled the ship with a lantern, too. But the ship did not answer. To this day, nobody is sure why this ship, the *Californian*, did not come to help the *Titanic*.

Now the captain knew that the ship was sinking and nobody could save it. "Load the lifeboats," he ordered. But there was a big problem. There were only enough lifeboats to carry 1,100 people—and there were more than twice that number on board! The captain had to save as many people as he could. "Women and children first!" he shouted.

Some women and children got into the lifeboats. They waved good-bye to their husbands and fathers. "See you in New York," the men called back, although they had little hope of it.

But a lot of people looked at those little boats so far down in the dark, icy water and thought, "The *Titanic* isn't going to sink. It's safer to stay here!" Many of the lifeboats were only half full.

By 1:00 in the morning, if you were standing on the deck of the *Titanic*, you could tell it really *was* going to sink. Because water was pouring into the front sections of the ship, it was tilting. People held on to posts and each other. Some men tied deck chairs together. They hoped to use them as rafts.

Finally, Captain Smith gave his crew one last order: "Every man for himself." Some stayed on the ship. Some jumped into the cold ocean.

Nobody is sure what happened to Captain Smith. Some say he went down with the ship. Others say he jumped into the water to save a baby. All we know for certain is that he did not survive.

The lifeboats rowed away from the ship. Some people covered their eyes so they wouldn't see the *Titanic* go down. They had family and friends on board. Other people watched. Maybe it wouldn't sink after all! The ship's lights were still on; the band was still playing.

At 2:20 in the morning of April 15, only two and a half hours after the *Titanic* hit the iceberg, there was a loud groaning sound. The ship broke into two pieces and sank two and a half miles to the bottom of the ocean.

The people in the lifeboats shivered in the night. How long would it be until help came? Would it come at all?

After more than an hour on the dark sea, a light appeared in the distance. Was it a ship coming to save them? People lit matches and set fire to scarves, scraps of paper, whatever they could find. They held up the torches to say, "Help us! We are here."

At last, they saw the *Carpathia*. Now they would be rescued! As the sun began to light up the sky, the survivors of the *Titanic* were pulled aboard the *Carpathia*. They were wet, cold, and very tired. But they were still alive! They would have much to tell about their ordeal. But for now, they would get warm clothes, hot food, and rest.

The sinking of the *Titanic* was a horrible disaster. Of the 2,224 people on board, only 705 lived.

Because of the fate of the *Titanic*, rules at sea were changed. Today ships must have enough lifeboats for every person on board, and enough binoculars for the crew. A ship's message room has to be operating all the time to answer SOS calls from other ships. There is now an ice patrol to warn ships about icebergs.

For seventy-three years, nobody knew where the *Titanic* was. Finally, in 1985, a team of scientists found the wreck. They used Alvin, an undersea robot, to explore it and take pictures. Then in 1996, another team of scientists used special equipment to "see" through layers of mud that cover the ship. They learned that the iceberg had made six very small holes. But those small holes were in just the wrong places. That is why the ship sank so fast.

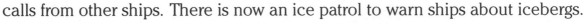

The *Titanic* still lies at the bottom of the ocean. Some people want to bring up her treasures—jewels, gold coins, old bottles of wine. Some French scientists already have raided the wreck. But most scientists want to leave the grave untouched. That shows respect for those who died. They also want to keep exploring the wreck. They want to uncover more mysteries of the greatest ship that ever sank, the *Titanic*.